THE CHILDREN'S GRIEF-MANAGEMENT BOOK

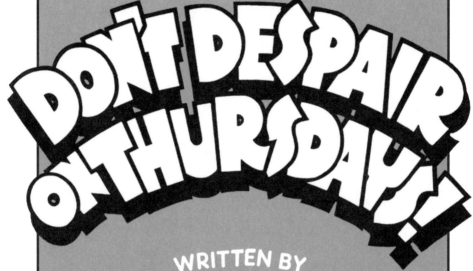

DON'T DESPAIR ON THURSDAYS!

WRITTEN BY

ADOLPH MOSER
Ed.D.

ILLUSTRATED BY

DAVID MELTON

LANDMARK EDITIONS, INC.
1904 Foxridge Drive • Kansas City, KS 66106 • www.landmarkeditions.com

Eighth Printing

TEXT COPYRIGHT © 1996 BY ADOLPH J. MOSER
ILLUSTRATIONS COPYRIGHT © 1996 BY DAVID MELTON

International Standard Book Number: 0-933849-60-5

Library of Congress Cataloging-in-Publication Data
Moser, Adolph, 1938-
    Don't despair on Thursdays! : the children's grief-management book / written by Adolph Moser :
illustrated by David Melton.
    p. cm.
    Summary: Examines, in simple text, how to deal with feelings of grief when people or pets
die, or when friends move away.
ISBN 0-933849-60-5
    1. Grief in children—Juvenile literature.
    2. Grief in adolescence—Juvenile literature.
    3. Bereavement in children—Juvenile literature.
    4. Bereavement in adolescence—Juvenile literature.
    [1. Grief.   2. Death.]

I. Melton, David, ill.   II. Title.
BF723.G75M68   1995   155.9'37'083—dc20   95-8653
                                                        CIP
                                                        AC

Editorial Coordinator: Nancy R. Thatch
Creative Coordinator: David Melton

Printed in the United States of America

Landmark Editions, Inc.
1904 Foxridge Drive
Kansas City, Kansas 66106
913-722-0700
www.landmarkeditions.com

Dedicated to
my mother
and to Kera,
who much too soon had to
learn to move beyond grief.

Dear Adult Reader:

Grieving is a serious experience for everyone, including children. After the loss of a relative, or a friend, or a pet, children may grieve much more intensely and much longer than many adults might suppose. Just because children are smaller than most adults does not mean that their grief is any smaller or less important than ours. The amount of grief a person feels cannot be determined by the weight, or the height, or the age of the griever.

While children grieve, they need all the love, consideration, and help adults can give to them. They also need good information that can assist them in accepting the loss and in dealing with the pain they feel. DON'T DESPAIR ON THURSDAYS! was written to help children understand how grief affects them and to offer ways by which they can cope with and finally overcome their emotional trauma.

I hope that no child will have to read this book by himself or herself. I hope a caring and loving adult will be sitting next to the child, and with that child, the adult will explore the pages of this book as often as the youngster needs or wishes to do so.

— Sincerely,
Adolph Moser

Dear Young Reader:

If you have lost a relative, or a friend, or a pet, you know the grief you feel can be very painful. DON'T DESPAIR ON THURSDAYS! was written and illustrated especially for you. The purpose of this book is to give you information about grief and to offer you ways that can help you cope with the pain you feel.

I hope you will not have to read this book without a caring and loving adult sitting beside you. But if you cannot find such an adult, then I would feel privileged if you would think of me as your adult friend and pretend that I am with you. Together, you and I can share these pages as often as you need to or want to do so.

— Your Friend,
Adolph Moser

It happens every day —
something changes.

Some of the changes
in our lives are good,
and they make us happy.

On our birthdays,
we are one year older.
To celebrate,
we have a party.

Our grandparents
come to visit,
and they bring presents.

We go on a picnic
with our parents
and have a wonderful time.

We become best friends
with someone we really like.

We get a new puppy.

We start to school
and learn new things.

But sometimes
there are bad changes in our lives,
and they make us sad.

Last week,
John's grandmother died.
He misses her smile
and her kind voice.

Susan's parents
got a divorce.
Now Susan lives
with her mother.
She sees her father
only on weekends.

But Susan feels
that she has lost
her father, and more.
She feels she has lost
her family, too.
She hopes her parents will
get together again.
But that hasn't happened,
and Susan is still sad.

Tom's best friend, Jeff,
moved away.
He moved to another town
that is located in another state.
Tom misses Jeff.
He feels it is almost
as if Jeff has died.

Now and then,
Tom talks to Jeff
on the telephone.
But that isn't the same
as seeing his friend in person.

Last week,
Jane's kitten ran out
into the street
and was hit by a car.

If the kitten had to die,
Jane was glad that he
was killed instantly
and that he didn't
have time to suffer.

When Jane buried the kitten's body,
she cried a lot.

She loved her kitten.
and she will miss him
for a long time.

When people or pets
we love die,
or when friends
move away,
we miss them,
and we grieve.

Grief is the
sadness and pain we feel
when we have lost
someone or something
we care about.

It is normal
for us to grieve.

When we grieve,
we sometimes cry.
Some people think only babies cry,
but that is not true.

Big burly truck drivers
sometimes cry.

So do sumo wrestlers.

Even champion muscle-builders
cry when they are sad.

When we are hurt or sad,
it can be good for us to cry.
Crying can help us relieve
some of the pain and sadness we feel.

After we cry,
we often feel better.

When people or pets
we love are gone,
we may wish we had done
more nice things for them
and said kinder words to them.

But we cannot
change the past.
Feeling guilty
for the things we did
or did not do in the past
doesn't help
anyone or anything.

Some people say, "Time heals everything."
They say, "In time you won't feel so sad."

But grieving doesn't
automatically stop
in a certain number
of days or weeks,
or months or years.

The grief you feel
may last for a long time.

Time alone does not stop your grief.

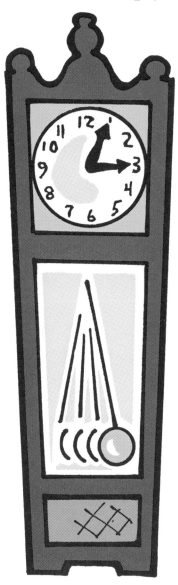

But time can
help you feel better
if you help yourself.

And there are ways
you can help yourself.

You can start by
admitting to yourself
that deep down inside
you feel a lot of pain.

It is good for you
to understand
that the pain you feel
is real,
and you are feeling
this pain NOW!

It is natural
for you to feel the pain.
And it is important for you
to take the time to grieve.

Some days your grief
may come and go.
One minute, you feel fine.

Then suddenly you think
about your loss,
and you are hit
by a "grief attack."

When a "grief attack" hits,
don't try to ignore it.
Stop whatever you're doing
and allow yourself
to feel the pain.

If you do,
your next "grief attack"
may not be quite so strong
or last as long.

Your grief can affect
your sleep, your appetite,
your moods, your behavior,
and your thinking.

Sometimes,
you can become so upset
and confused
that you may wonder
if you are losing your mind.

But you are not
LOSING YOUR MIND.
You are
USING YOUR MIND.

Your mind is working for you.
It is trying to help you
accept your grief
and adjust to the loss you feel.

Even when your sadness and pain
are at their very worst,
        DON'T DESPAIR!

Despair means to give up hope.
Don't do that!
NEVER GIVE UP HOPE!

42

Remember —
at one time or another,
most people lose
someone or something
they love.
They feel the pain of grief,
but they survive.

You will survive, too.
So hold on to your hope.

To help you live through
your time of grief,
write a message to yourself.

On a notecard
or on a piece of paper,
Write —

Then, place that message
in your pocket
or in your billfold,
and carry it with you
at all times.

All day long
on Thursdays,
if a "grief attack" hits —

Pull out the message
and read —

This message
will remind you
not to give up hope.

Don't keep your grief to yourself.
Tell someone you trust
about the sadness and pain you feel.

Talk to your father
or your mother.

Or talk to your teacher,
or your school counselor,
or to a friend.

If you need a hug,
ask for one.

Writing can help relieve your grief.

If you think of nice things
you wish you had said
to the person or the pet you have lost,
write a letter to him or her
and say those nice things.
Then put the letter in
a special box or drawer.

Or write a few paragraphs
that tell how you felt
about that person or pet.

Or write about some of the
happy times you had together.

Or you may even want to write
about how the person or pet died
or went away.

Drawing or painting can help, too.

Draw or paint some pictures
that show some of the things
you remember about
the person or pet you have lost.

Look at photographs of the person or pet.

Some of the pictures
may bring tears to your eyes.
But it may surprise you
to find that other pictures
may make you smile.

When you have
made your way through Thursday,
congratulate yourself.

Then turn over your notecard
and add —

Remember —
each day
that you accept
the grief you feel,
and you don't despair,
you will be one day better.

There are no shortcuts
through your grief.
Your time of grieving
should not be rushed.
You have to live through it,
one day at a time.

The sadness you feel
may never completely go away,
but if you accept your grief
and allow your feelings to happen,
the sadness and pain you feel
will begin to lessen.

One day, you will be able to
read the things you've written,
look at the drawings you've made,
and see the photographs you've kept
without feeling so much pain.

You will be able to
to go on with your life —
you will make new friends,
care about other people,
and enjoy other pets.

So —

DON'T DESPAIR ON THURSDAYS,

> or on Fridays,
> or on any other day.
> Hold on to your hope,
> and your time of grief
> will pass.

EMOTIONAL IMPACT SERIES

Children love these books because they help children deal with real problems that they face every day.

Counselors, teachers, and parents appreciate the practical advice these books offer to the youngsters who are in their care.

These Outstanding Books Are Highly Recommended

Much-needed books!
I enthusiastically recommend all of them to parents, teachers, clinicians, and, of course, to children.
> — Theodore Tollefson, Ph.D. Clinical Psychologist

Delightful and practical!
You don't have to be a psychologist to read these books to a child. Better still, have a child read them to you.
> — Larry M. Hubble, Ph.D. Psychologist

What helpful books for teaching children important methods of self-control. I highly recommend them!
> — Suzanne Leiphant, Ph.D. Clinical Psychologist & Author

Informative, compassionate, wise!
These helpful handbooks clearly explain and entertain at the same time.
> — Dr. Taylor McGee, HSPP Child Psychologist

One only has to read today's headlines or hear the news to realize how much these books are needed.
> — Phyllis Morrison Grateful Parent

These are very important books.
I have no doubt they could help save the lives of many children and adults, too.
> — R.M. Fortrell, Ph.D. Psychologist